Surviving The Stain of Losing My First Love

By

Ollie Marshall-Rico

Copyright 2022 Ollie Marshall-Rico

Published in the United States of America

Paperback ISBN (978-1-959960-11-9)
Hardcover ISBN (978-1-959960-12-6)

Ollie Marshall-Rico
440 Central Avenue
Orange, New Jersey 07050-2502 the USA

Rights Permission
For Book Rights Adaptation and other Rights Permission.
Call (973) 699-3808
Website: www.olliemarshallbooks9.com
Email: olliemarshallrico@yahoo.com

INTRODUCTION

This is my story, "From My Side of The Fence."

This is the only story I know to tell. When you read this book, let it not be from someone you respected as a sister, auntie, or teacher but rather, "A true heartache get together a night out with the girls." A night that I never had because the pain was deeply buried in a grave. Only now have I opened up that grave to be whole as a person, five-decade gone.

If there is a lesson in this story, especially to a young reader, do not allow yourself to fall into a hopeless trap as I had many years gone. I speak now not of my present situation but of guys with great morals who never had an inch of a chance into my heart because my heart still had the stain of my first lost love. I had a coffin buried deep that I had to self-dig up. What caused me to dig up this grave at this moment in time? The loss of my firstborn, not biologically, but a child who came into my life early. The voice of his last spoken words still rings in my ears. "Mom, I don't know what I would do without you. I couldn't live without you." I would immediately buff that saying, "I don't ever want to hear those words coming from your mouth. Can you imagine how sad that would make me, knowing you were not going on happily with your life?" In ending that conversation, I would say, "I love you." He would say, 'I love you more." I would say, "I love you most." He would then point both arms in my direction, saying, "I love you most of the most." I would laugh, saying, "I guess I can't beat that." We would then laugh, and he would point both arms at me again as he would laugh, walking away. Therefore, I think my son is carrying me as I write these words, although the day will come soon. I hope to close his gravesite to know his body has left this earthly world. I know I must take this step, and I will soon. My husband, friends, and the Almighty have helped me walk this final journey in accepting this reality.

My mother gave birth to ten boys. I don't know the reality of their love life related to women. I hope their respect for women went more profound than I experienced with Nathan. Again, I say this story comes from my side of the fence. I don't know Nathan's story; I don't even know whether he has one related to me. Perhaps I grew up in a shielded world; my brothers were always my protectors as I grew up; therefore, I never experienced a genuine girl-boyfriend relationship before Nathan. Virginity was always treasured in my family. It was to be issued only to the one you marry. In releasing my virginity to Nathan, I naturally thought it was a lifetime commitment. Not knowing, I was just one of many within his treasure box. I was a country girl from the back woods, deep Ozark, dumber than dumbest. In fairness to country girls, they are more aware than I was then.

As these words flow through these lines, please do not be too harsh on Nathan or me because his actions demonstrated that I should have run away from him the first time he wrote me with another person's name. But as he explained it, I was ignorant and crazy enough to believe it. His words were truthful, even if he changed them from one moment to the next. As I reflect now, perhaps he was telling me to go away from him, and I could not make that move. Therefore, my emotions were completely out of control. To survive, perhaps that is why I had to bury those emotions within a grave. We all have made choices, and I did what I thought was necessary at the time. Yes, it was hard holding on day by day. I had pride within myself but couldn't turn Nathan's thoughts away.

A time that laid buried until this day…this is my naked rawness.

Contents

SECTION I

VIRGINITY GONE

This story looks at my one-time virginity, a period of innocence. At the time, I was exposed to someone who took it. I had misinterpreted the sign as love. It was my first encounter with sex.

It began one night when Nathan tried to have sex with me for the first time, which was impossible. He spoke these kind words to me. "We will not make love tonight because your body is not physically ready, and I don't want your body. I want your mind too."

I misinterpreted that statement to think Nathan truly loved me, knowing that he realized I was an eighteen-year-old virgin and I had to be physically prepared to have sex with him. He had some cream he used that elevated the sensation of the act itself the next time. Although it was pretty painful, from that day onwards, I craved Nathan; for approximately four months, Nathan had me in any way he desired, and I loved it. It was a sad day when I had to return home to Arkansas to finish my last year of high school. I cried as he held me close. He consoled me, saying, "one year is not that long. Soon you will return to California to go to college, and I will be here waiting for you with open arms."

The following year, I returned to California on the Greyhound Bus. The bus took me downtown to Los Angeles Bus Depot. As I reflected on it, my brother-in-law was a few minutes late picking me up at the bus station. I must have looked lost because a well-dressed man walked up and attempted to assist me, just as my brother-in-law called out my name. He later shared this with my sister, saying, "A pimp almost picked up your sister." I said, "That was a nice man who appeared to be a preacher. He was asking me if he could help me." The stranger said, "You appear to be lost."

I was a country girl exposed to some of the elements of the city for the very first time. I strongly lacked the knowledge that people living within the country's boundaries have today. This was a well-dressed man who I thought was a preacher. Instead, he was a pimp, as my brother-in-law described, hanging around the bus station looking for runaways to become a part of his circle.

Shortly afterward, I met Nathan through a family member. He was friendly and bookish. He later went to UCLA and Berkley, where he received his Ph.D. in Physics after leaving junior college. He was academically gifted with words, which impressed me greatly. Years later, he could have been+ a ditch digger, and I would have gladly bathed his aching feet at night to have him near me. Maybe it was because he had been the first to enter my vagina. He stopped working at Douglas Aircraft in California when he started school at UCLA.

When I first met Nathan that summer, he was a couple of years older than me. He often took me around his family, especially around his oldest sister. I enjoyed this tremendously. He loved his family, and he chaired his nephews and nieces. However, he loved his baby niece Val, who was a cute little flower. Besides spending time with his family, we spent time in cheap motels having sex. This was all new to me, and I loved every bit of it. I thought we would be together for life. My imagination ran wild rapidly. When I departed for Arkansas, I took Nathan in my dreams.

Returning to California one year later, things had changed. Reality had hit me square in the face. One thing that was difficult for me to comprehend was that he was not mature enough to sit me down to explain that his feelings toward me had altered, or he just had discarded me as the woman in the street who had not been paid for her previous sexual encounters and did not deserve any form of an explanation. I was indeed in a whirlwind.

SECTION I
POEMS

The Stone

Disappeared

Denied

Pest

Baby Bottom Clear

The Encounter

The Glowing Present

Stomach

Country Girl

The Bed

No Return

Searching

THE STONE

A stone knocked on my door yesterday.
I let it in because I thought it was cotton
It meshed me into pieces; perhaps it did not even know.
It became the last as well as the first.
Innocent eyes were hopeless, casket closed.
The stone left a life's tone with its own set of memories.

DISAPPEARED

You were the sunshine that I exhibited.
You were the reason I dreamed.
I could not or would not perceive a season without you in my arms.
You were my future.
There wasn't anything else to nurture when it came to you.
Beyond you, there was not a tomorrow.
Cold, no, you were not only my hot tea but my complete package.
Except for one day, I went to sleep.
When I awakened, you were not there anymore.

DENIAL

Yes, Geek, physics brain stuck in the rain.
What did I ever see in you?
Except, well, you were my first.
Oh, my drain allowed your plunger to go into my vein.

Yes, Geek, physics brain stuck in the rain.
Compared to yonder years, where was my mind?
Yesterday, I ran to you with open space.
Today, I am trying to honor my feeling with new birth.

Yes, Geek, physics brain stuck in the rain.
Without a thought of destruction, I allowed you to enter my castle.
Your emotions are technical, structured, caged, and bagged on an electrical current.
With you, I danced on feeling and perceived you on emotions.

Yes, Geek, physics brain stuck in the rain.
Ditch-Digger or CEO or anyone else, it was always you in my eyes.
What was it that clinched me?
Was it your geeky personality or the first time you denied yourself the pleasure of
sex with me?

PEST

They called it puppy love.
Now, tell me, why has it not grown into a complete dog?
Yes, it was my first; first, I stand to tell.
It still stands now, refusing to dissipate or resolve itself.

They called it puppy love.
If so, it should have outgrown itself.
For years, I have sought to put it to rest.
But that pest keeps nibbling at the door, refusing to allow that door to be closed.

They called it puppy love.
Was it to consume itself in time?
They said it would go just as water dissipates in the sun.
It is a legend that is repeatedly shared.

They called it puppy love.
One day that puppy became lost in the trenches, unable to find its way out.
The puppy was exposed to many, yet not able to see one.
Perhaps the searchers became bored and discarded it.

BABY BOTTOM CLEAR

Morning came, evening came, night came, and the pain did not stop.
An acknowledgment would not come this day or the next.
His sibling echoed; the disease I had planted in him had rung from his mouth.
Cried I to sister kin, "he had been my only; virginity he took without a thought.

Morning came, evening came, night came, and the pain did not stop.
An acknowledgment would not come this day or the next.
It mattered not; the test came back clear as a baby's bottom.
Salty to the womb, brother's voice face echoed on someone short of drowning.

Morning came, evening came, night came, and the pain did not stop.
An acknowledgment would not come this day or the next.
I don't know whether he loved me or not; I did hope so.
Taking one's virginity only to pleasure oneself without thought is unthinkable.

Morning came, evening came, night came, and the pain did not stop.
An acknowledgment would not come this day or the next.
At last, a revelation has freed me; I can now walk with the freedom of the past.
Mind freedom, your touch remains; you were my first.

THE ENCOUNTER

How did our sexual acts turn into my lifetime memory?
You probably wouldn't remember; it was the time we attempted our first sexual
encounter.

I was unable to greet your desire because of my virginity.
A world filled with sex, perceived as real love, a body yielding for more each time
we engaged.

Your objective became my dream; your reality was my reality; I alone merged into
you, not you into me.
Time would escape, but you would remain in my heart deeply as ever, distance
manner not.

You sent me a poem with another person's name; perhaps that was your truth.
Unfortunately, I was too naïve to recognize it; your explanation smoothly
explained it away.

With a smile, I took it all in without question.
A lifetime is perceived based upon a first-time sexual encounter.

Years went by, and people danced through my world until, one day, a volcano
erupted.
A volcano erupted, and a burst of buried rock layers melted into dusk's sand.

Now, I can openly say you were indeed the love of my life, but I, not yours.

THE GLOWING PRESENT

What a beautiful present it was wrapped like sunshine.
The box was bright with a glowing light.
The present was complete, all one wanted in a glance.
Nothing could alter it; it would have gleamed in a mud gale.

What a beautiful present it was wrapped like sunshine.
It was gloriously glittering in the perfect summation
The bow was flawless.
The box was small, but the mind was taller than the highest mountain.

What a beautiful present it was wrapped like sunshine.
Our souls met once, and each appeared to be pure as gold.
Without an explanation, one soul turned into a mold.
I refused to fold and went to seek the why and why not, but none came.

What a beautiful present it was wrapped like sunshine.
A world to cope now felt beyond the slightest hope.
Survival mobility interplayed with thoughts that ran high.
The focus now had to be on normality among the living.

STOMACH

Why is my stomach cramping?
It bleeds, trying to escape the pain running through my veins.
The soreness has cramped me into a ball against the wall.
My thoughts of you have anchored me into self-denial.

Why is my stomach cramping?
Medicines have sought to put this agony of pain at rest.
Trying to inch forward, yet moving three steps backward.
Fantasyland must come into reality to move forward.

Why is my stomach cramping?
Yesterday is gone; reality never was in play.
Yet, my mind continues to sway back and forward.
Is this mind in a cult state?

Why is my stomach cramping?
The body breathes with the mind.
Let me connect and bind them all into one.
A world of outer beauty is crying and waiting for self to come into reality.

COUNTRY GIRL

The country girl went to the city, not knowing the grasp aches to follow.
She encountered a legacy that brought her to her knees.
The palm trees were not long enough to contain the stacked blood piles.
Miles of flood water dripped from her face.

The country girl went to the city, not knowing the grasp aches to follow.
A once innocent mind would shoelace into insanity.
She has encountered many, but none laced the ladder step as one
She was hung with thread from the tallest rocky mountain.

The country girl went to the city, not knowing the grasp aches to follow.
Doors would open and close, but none held her centered as the desired one.
Aches were shelved to cope and survive the rock-pounding flesh memories.
The weeds were trying desperately to find a way up the rocky mountain.

The country girl went to the city, not knowing the grasp aches to follow.
It was a world filled with clouds that shaded out the lights.
When lights appeared, the heart bellowed out in pain.
Yet, she moved like a lion while voices danced out her aches in shades of a
whisper.

THE BED

There were days the bed became my savior.
It rescued me when I needed it.
It comforted and delivered me into a world of silent cries.
A selfish prayer echoed from my lips.

There were days the bed became my savior.
I thought it was the destruction of me, not having you.
I could not see; it was not to be.
God's mercy had me in his grace at that time.

There were days the bed became my savior.
Reality came, and I proceeded with life.
Each step became a journey.
Tasks of survival moved on with mandatory chores.

There were days the bed became my savior.
It was me who suffered while you went on with your glorious life.
I tried to excavate the created dream I had of you.
But you were my crept crawler, beyond my control.

NO RETURN

The atmosphere was warm with some skeptical minds.
The room was crowded with patients' little smiles.
The pain was pounding in my stomach.
This pain would disappear but not the ache in my heart.

The atmosphere was warm with some skeptical minds.
I felt like crying, but the tears wouldn't come.
I am alone, not a soul to share my inner depth.
Tomorrow will come, and I will be emptier and loner than this day.

The atmosphere was warm with some skeptical minds.
People were coming and going.
My time had not arrived to go behind the curtains.
People are always making choices, I included.

The atmosphere was warm with some skeptical minds.
My most excellent thought had hung on this moment.
Beyond this date, there will be no return; it will always dance in my head,
How will my psyche come to gripe beyond the point of no return?

SEARCHING

My mind has gone searching for your presence of you.
Was it the time you denied yourself an intimate encounter?
Was the attempt too painful for you, or was I just too small for you to enter?
Perhaps that was the first time I saw you as a future mate.

My mind has gone searching for your presence of you.
The absence of you has made me go wondering endlessly.
Was it your hug embraced that security me from the world, I thought?
Had you stolen my mind with your geeky brilliance?

My mind has gone searching for your presence of you.
To open tomorrow's door, the essence of me must bring this to a close.
Are you far distant in the past, never to be resurrected?
Time has elapsed since that great or unforgivable misunderstood summer.

My mind has gone searching for your presence of you.
Am I searching for the warmth and secure feeling of your arms?
Was it the feeling of completeness when we finally cemented intimacy?
Am I searching for the depth of me?

SECTION II

ENTERING INTO A VALLEY OF MEMORY

Within two weeks after I had returned home, I received a poem from Nathan titled "Christy." He expressed his profound love for Christy. When I spoke with Nathan concerning the poem titled "Christy," I stated, "It's a nice poem, but it's entitled "Christy," and my name is Ollie." He said, " I was thinking of you when I wrote that poem, but I entitled it, Christy." How happy that made me. I went to school sharing the knowledge that "my boyfriend" had written me a poem. I must say, the poem titled Christy and not Ollie did bother me. A valley of thoughts created a void in my heart. It appeared I couldn't see beyond those acts of sexual encounters between Nathan and myself. This always took me into a deep valley when I thought of the name situation.

Returning home, my friends remained the same but on a different level. The young teenager who always fancied me went through my father to court me. He teased me after I had spent time babysitting my cousin in California. There wasn't an eye to view another after Nathan. Ken, who cared deeply for me, said, "You went to California and completely forgot about me. Who is this, Nathan, anyway? I would smile because I was in memory heaven.

At eighteen, I had never kissed a boy before Nathan. I dreamed of that first meeting with Nathan when I returned to California. But somehow, that first imagined meeting because a further distance. I went to school and ignored all the advances that came my way from other males. Nathan was my complete memory bank. He had been the light in my tunnel, and now that tunnel light was disappearing, as was he.

POEMS IN SECTION II

Me, Myself, and I

Dignity First

The Claimed

The Greatest Valley

Skeleton Face

Unpleasantness

Frozen Time

Softly Please

Suppression

You

Nightmare

Selfless Denial

The Common One

Resemble

ME, MYSELF, AND I

It was as though it was yesterday.
Distance had denied its cure.
A thousand miles had not removed the flame from the scored dissert.
The balcony roared with accolades.

It was as though it was yesterday.
Three yokes put it not at rest.
Time had gone untouched as if it were the first moment.
Decades stood on the first of innocent.

It was as though it was yesterday.
It was not a control button that could be turned on or off.
Time had elapsed, but only one remained in that twilight zone.
The zone heart had been stone fastened.

It was as though it was yesterday.
The people geared with laughter while one stood status still.
It was a moment of self-truth.
The acknowledgment had to come with self-awareness, inspired by other
condemnation.

It was as though it was yesterday.
The barrel was bottom bare, yet, the heart pounded still.
There was nothing there, nothing.
The walls of the time zone echoed on days gone, dream on, hitched on one's false
memories.

It was as though it was yesterday.
One desired escape wounded, not by choice.
Who would choose a mental state of agony?
Soon, will distance come with a release pill?

It was as though it was yesterday.
The pain of it was like insomnia.
It was like the mighty Mississippi River claiming unwanted, lost prey.
This is a prey calling all strength and power to endure survival.

It was as though it was yesterday.

The time of reckoning was forced upon this unwanted running soul.

A benediction could not be written, but this inner volcano turmoil had to be dealt with openly.

It was about me, myself, and my health that had to come with openness.

DIGNITY FIRST

Dignity, let me not give up.
It has been a talking box, "Where is my survival tool."
You do not understand, but I do.
The bell could toll for me, where dignity had escaped, that I know.

Dignity, let me not give up.
You smiled and made your jokes here and there through others.
Do you not know your jokes have mocked my being?
You loved me not; my mind has finally registered it.

Dignity, let me not give up.
You smiled and tried to embrace me with the thought of sex.
You know, it was only my running thoughts that were pure and innocent.
Your mind clenched me, yet you tormented me when our paths met.

Dignity, let me not give up.
What would you have done if I had taken you upon your tormented acts?
Perhaps laugh more resounding; seriously, I don't know.
I am hollow inside; you cannot or wish not to see.

Dignity, let me not give up.
Do I have any dignity left with this one-sided past raw sexual relationship?
It must be buried beyond six feet deep; excavation must come.
Unearth it, flush to the surface, although the raw truth will put me in a pickle jar.

Dignity, let me not give up.
I can go forward with your true thoughts now that I have accepted reality.
I can breathe with this pain implanted in me.
I breathe with the past, an opened counselor's door.
You made me care for you on the date you delayed taking my virginity.
My virginity was strong in my mind; my father had directed this road.

THE CLAIMED

Today, someone claimed my memories as I shared the Plato of my life.
How can that be?
I thought those memories were boxed, unique, and different from all others.
Could it be that we are all globally connected in trying to find the epitome of
happiness with the one who first struck the chord?

Today, someone claimed my memories as I shared the Plato of my life.
How can you steal someone's story when you never pasture that someone's
meadow?
Yet, she claimed my story.
How can that be?

Today, someone claimed my memories as I shared the Plato of my life.
Those are my memories.
They are the floral uniqueness of my world.
Why are you stealing my memories?

Today, someone claimed my memories as I shared the Plato of my life.
Those were my unique pain, cries of sorrow, and thoughts of endlessness.
How can my memories be your memories?
Are we globally connected in uniqueness?

THE GREATEST VALLEY

I have to have my say today, although it may mean nothing to you!
I am a world of make-believe, a cracked-up world of love, the crack demon armed
and unreachable.
A crack head may say there isn't a perception beyond the crack that kills the
moment craved.
A reality moment appeared, a reflection upon what had escaped in the
cracked-up body.

I have to have my say today, although it may mean nothing to you!
The feeling I have has to be demonized.
Now, what is that?
A life self-destructed based upon unrealistic love that I created, grave planted.

I have to have my say today, although it may mean nothing to you!
I selected to maintain the steps that once crossed my pasture.
I could not see because I had allowed myself to be demonized.
Is it to have felt the consumption of love once or not at all, tell me?

I have to have my say today, although it may mean nothing to you!
Was it ever a time when I was the queen of all?
If, I ask myself, was it worse than the years of pain?
Today it is a hole more profound than the most incredible valley.

SKELETON FACE

The skeleton has finally risen for its face.
How can I make amends to myself?
Years denied, acknowledged, not your life impacted.
Double-covered full moon when it fought like a bull to stay in the light.

The skeleton has finally risen for its face.
`How can I make amends to myself?
Was it a skill coped with bringing another day?
But why was it so long?

The skeleton has finally risen for its face.
`How can I make amends to myself?
Silk face, years covered, had become stone layered without tone.
A hole opened to bury me, but it blossomed into tulips that had laid years dominant.

The skeleton has finally risen for its face.
`How can I make amends to myself?
Years element, gone unrecoverable.
Let me breathe the new while knowledge is viewed to guide the future with wisdom.

UNPLEASANTNESS

The purest soul leaped off a mountain without anyone to catch it.
It beeped mercifully, but not one reached to comfort or heard the cry.
The cry dry because her mate had another matching date.
That could not be grasped, so years went buried in halls of walls.

The purest soul leaped off a mountain without anyone to catch it.
Memory lane scrapped thoughts of the past.
Would that last forever?
The day of reckoning would come when his wall would fall, sadly, say.

The purest soul leaped off a mountain without anyone to catch it.
The tomb buried was there to stay; the dark hour came and went.
The mornings were pushed into the night, and nights were made into the morning.
Trouble heart experiences had to be eradicated from memories.

The purest soul leaped off a mountain without anyone to catch it.
Cope changes had laced dances in and out of this world.
But none would sing a true light that had sighted a bright light gone.
Through this light, one had to unbury all the unpleasantness that had held such
sadness.

FROZEN TIME

You crossed my mind today.
These broken frames should not hold yesterday's memories.
Yet those thoughts have frozen in time.
Today's memories should not ride on falsehood.
My silent thoughts often echo your name.

SOFTLY PLEASE

The uncanny person trudges upon others.
You are elevating inner thoughts, thinking only of yourself.
We are eliminating the worth of another, self-motivated.
Delicate glass has been broken.
Mending may occur, but the original state equals not.
Trudges softly and dances effortlessly with the door you open.

SUPPRESSION

Part of me had escaped, and I stood unaware of the past.
Where have my memories gone?
Have they deleted me?
Buried deep, my thoughts cried out to be recused.

Part of me had escaped, and I stood unaware of the past.
Buried deep, the safety shield has thoughts of exclusion.
I was stripped naked; my consciousness was stolen.
I had to be put into a different atmosphere to claim another day.

Part of me had escaped, and I stood unaware of the past.
You were my basket; you had the goodies; I left them willingly with you.
You were my oppressor, too; this mind was unjustly yours.
I had to create a dense mechanism to remove myself from your consciousness.

Part of me had escaped, and I stood unaware of the past.
You were no longer welcome in my conscious.
I wanted to remove memories from my conscious, painful awareness ones.
You are a part of me forever, the good and the bad; my conscious has mastered you
into it.

YOU

You were my love.
You were my sanity.
You were who I was.
You were my entire existence.
You were the bread that fed me.
You were my change.
.You were my worries.
You were cries of darkness.
You were the depth of my soul.
You were what I once was and no more.
You were a love that I once had and held on to mercifully.
You were the rape of my soul.
You were everything that I once was and wasn't.
You were the laughter in me.
You were the pity of me that had hung over a rocky mountain.
You were the beauty of my soul that allowed me to understand emptiness,
You were my failures.
You were my sleepless nights.
You were my rooted pains.
You were my default success.
You were my lungs in a breathless cave.
I was the venom that had stolen my life through you.
Through you, I had forgotten who I was, the whole of me.

NIGHTMARE

Decades ago, he left without a goodbye.
He had chosen another, and you are still in a nightmare.
A person has a right to follow his own heart.
Did I not deserve a sit-down farewell?
I guess not; those were his thoughts of you.

SELFLESS DENIAL

The pain of it, he married another, divorced, and you went to share his bed.
It had been decades, and I still dreamed and lived in yesteryears.
It wasn't what I wanted, but it claimed me anyway.
Did I cheat myself, or did I go with my heart?

The pain of it, he married another, divorced, and you went to share his bed.
Time has come and gone a trillion times.
A glimpse of this present was sought.
He desired me not.

The pain of it, he married another, divorced, and you went to share his bed.
Did I know my self-worth?
I refused to let the road path guide me.
Swimming in yesterday's dream that has repeatedly escaped me.

The pain of it, he married another, divorced, and you went to share his bed.
It has stagnated with a lost love that will never become a reality.
Zombie walking shoes without self-worth.
I am trying to free this doormat mind.

THE COMMON ONE

I am the common one.
I am a Good Will Item that has been discarded.
Where is my place?
Just for one spot I seek, a place to call my own.
I am the common one.

RESEMBLE

Lost love may sometimes resemble death.
What can you do?
Will you stand while the sunshine turns into clouds?
Will you turn into coal in a fire?
What will comfort and sustain you?
Will you move forward to grow yourself?

SECTION III

UN-COCOON FALSE LOVE

I began to drift into existence. Hours drifted into days, and days drifted into weeks. My whole world was absolutely nothing without the thought of Nathan. I couldn't believe he was ignoring me, not returning my calls. When we finally met, it was for his needs, sex only, and it was no longest a privilege for me. My body was used only for masturbation as we connected. When he was aroused and unable to satisfy his needs elsewhere, I was always available. I slept and forced myself to continue to go to school; that was my whole world.

One day Nathan called me and said he wanted to see me; overjoyed was I; until he looked me in the face and said I had given him chlamydia. I was dumber than the dumbest. I called my oldest sister to tell her what Nathan had told me. I couldn't even clearly pronounce this sexual disease that I had supposedly transmitted. She immediately picked me up and took me to the doctor.

Although the test result was negative, I still pounded for Nathan. How foolish I was. That I know was insane, yet it is the bare truth. He must have related this untruth to one of his siblings. Because when I encountered one brother several months later, he openly told me that I had given Nathan chlamydia. I stood there with tears welling in my eyes, speechless, mumbling that my test was negative. This sibling must have felt a sense of my pain at that moment. He said, "That's all in the past; let's forget about it." As he walked away. I stumbled, trying desperately not to fall. At that moment, I felt a sense of worthlessness. My survival skills were on edge. I went to bed and curled up into a ball…tears rolled down my cheeks. There I stayed until it was time for me to prepare for school. My sense of living was none.

Time slowly drifted on, and I endured it, neglecting myself when it came to committing to any males with great morals. For example, Jessie was a person who wanted to date me, but I refused. Before Jessie went to the University of Chicago to receive his Ph.D., he tried to get engaged to me. That was insane because I had not even kissed Jessie. He was like a big brother. I always talked with Jessie when we attended junior college. I never shared my thoughts about Nathan. Years later, Jessie because the Chairman of a Black Study Department in one of California's Universities. I was unable to move on as an average person. Psychologically my mind was truly messed-up. My oldest sister had guys from her church lined up to date me, but I refused to consider one.

My family surrounding me must not have known the inner pain I was going through because I never discussed Nathan with them. I always had a beautiful front to display to my family. As I was attending junior college, I lived with an extended family member, Aunt Everette, who went to work every day. When I was closed up in my room, she thought I was studying and praised me for studying hard. The front I displayed was always there around my family; I did not want them to know the inner pain of my heart and soul.

POEMS IN SECTION III

Time Zone

Eyes That Kill

Eyes

Mixed Emotion

The Lost Heart

Sour

Is It Time

Lost Love

Parasites

The Paradox

Hidden Intrusion

Secret

Haze

Your Way

Smelling Green

TIME ZONE

It was the day of reckoning.
Many years had escaped, and I was caught in a time zone.
Was it shock therapy?
Mind healing must come.
Suddenly, I moved about me, alone.
My mind game was no more, the games of self-survival.
I had built my cocoon of skills.
The summer false and real encounter had to be opened up.

EYES THAT KILL

Not even a spoken word crept from those lips.
What did I ever do to you?
You looked at me without a smile as words peeled from my lips.
I wandered here and there in silence and danced my feet across the room.

Not even a spoken word crept from those lips.
What did I ever do to you?
Do you hate me without a cause?
Or is it a cause unknown to me?

Not even a spoken word crept from those lips.
What did I ever do to you?
Please hold me up this day, Lord.
I need to be held; I am struggling inside, trying to keep it together.

Not even a spoken word crept from those lips.
What did I ever do to you?
What had questionable which eyes hung on me…a monster?
Your lips were glued tightly, and your eyes viewed me from head to toe.

Not even a spoken word crept from those lips.
What did I ever do to you?
Sister kin, he had eyes that would kill.
Not one spoken word crept from those lips; only detectable eyes spoke that day.

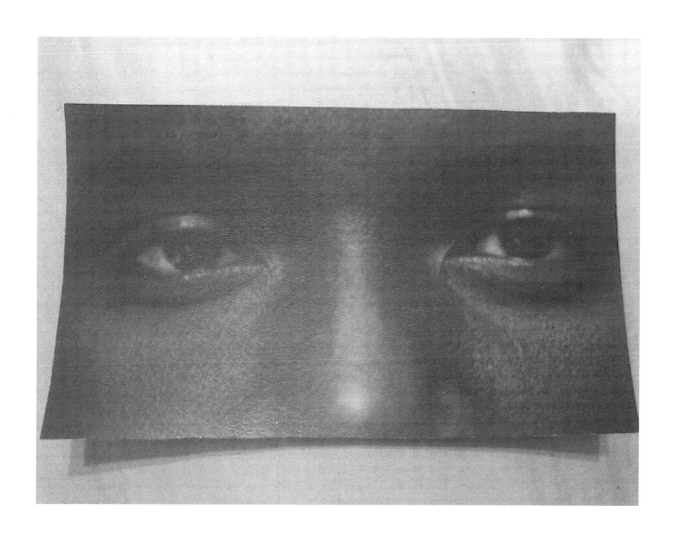

EYES

My eyes have opened to see the greatness at times as the darkness.
What has brought this into my sight?
Perhaps it was the years of nights I had eyes seeing not?
Was it the actual stump that opened my toes into wounds?

My eyes have opened to see the greatness at times as the darkness.
What has brought this into my sight?
Were they faces that came into all colors?
Was it the elite that had pranced through my world whose voices sought to belittle?

My eyes have opened to see the greatness at times as the darkness.
What has brought this into my sight?
Each was singing their songs.
We each had marched but to a different drummer.

My eyes have opened to see the greatness at times as the darkness.
What has brought this into my sight?
Life never stops; we must catch on to the beat of it.
.One heart stops in a moment, but another one opens up.

MIXED EMOTIONS

I cry or yield not for you, my love, but me.
Are you judgmental? Who has not walked a smooth pathway?
A mind opened with a bit of light for the other to share.
I can organize the essence of my beauty when it is at my ankles low.

I cry or yield not for you, my love, but me.
The day my heart beats on a different throne.
You claimed heart, but just not this way.
Your memories will always ankle in my heart without control.

I cry or yield not for you, my love, but me.
Our departure has come, but my heart still peels for your warmth.
We each had a way but never to be bound as one yoke.
Your memories still pound in me, but without the yo-yo.

I cry or yield not for you, my love, but me.
I paced when you laced a different path.
There was not a sight in me with your total departure with another.
My hopes had finally dissipated in the wind.

THE LOST HEART

Twenty-four-seven, who held one breath for me, not one.
Selflessness went on with great expectation to heighten one's own life.
Ping pong balls lit the room as each marched on with penetrated steps.
The beating of the heart came and when.

Twenty-four-seven, who held one breath for me, not one.
Friends, no, space embraced the wind of your firing cry.
Only the trapper knows who speaks not.
You bleed, bleed on; your choice has long gone!

Twenty-four-seven, who held one breath for me, not one.
Perfect, not you; let it be, let it be.
Your soul will always cry; that is the essence of you.
The angel of mercy resting in God's hands.

Twenty-four-seven, who held one breath for me, not one.
Roads are blended with many curves that the eyes see not.
The heart that never came to beat has been cemented in your thoughts.
So let it be, let it be; the peace perhaps lies in God's hands.

SOUR

Is it unique, unique within itself?
Do I stand alone?
Hope like a dope fringe; my dream will turn into yours?
Hoping the never-ending lemon will turn into a sweet pie.

Is it unique, unique within itself?
Do I stand alone?
Hill events are isolated with an icy chill; I dare not think beyond this point.
I hoped this mind would be bound towards my steps when the sky opened.

Is it unique, unique within itself?
Do I stand alone?
It was a game of another, although it may have been lame.
You have been caught up high without a net below.

Is it unique, unique within itself?
Do I stand alone?
Unable to free oneself; frozen thoughts after counting to a hundred.
The ounces pile up, and the ball bounces without a catcher on the mound.

IS IT TIME?

It is what it is, and life goes on.
Sometimes we sigh or cry when death calls.
Sometimes we stand mute with our thoughts.
Sometimes we feel relieved that our loved one is finally resting peacefully.

It is what it is, and life goes on.
Sometimes we mount with the belief that morning has finally come with our
departed one.
Sometimes we encounter elements in others we thought not.
Sometimes morning comes, and everything becomes too powerful to cope with at
that moment.

It is what it is, and life goes on.
Sometimes people want control factors, but there are none there.
Sometimes we wonder where and when, but we know not.
Sometimes it creeps without beeps, or it may have its longevity.

It is what it is, and life goes on.
Sometimes we procrastinate and deny that the date has been issued to each that
breathes.
Sometimes when that moment comes, the best or the worst occurs in one's
behavior.
Sometimes it provides light to those who once walked and talked in darkness.

It is what it is, and life goes on.
Don't freeze; morning will come, and night will disappear.
You will be or not be in the midst of one of four seasons.
Will you melt in the walls of the past, walking lifeless, breathing not?

"IT IS TIME"

LOST LOVE

How can one lose a love that they never possessed?
It is a deception of one's mind.
It is a game created through one's fantasy.
It's not even a puppy love state.

How can one lose a love that they never possessed?
It is a self-render act on one's party.
While another connects as one's first experience.
One is filled with fantasy, while another sees himself as the conquered one.

How can one lose a love that they never possessed?
A toddler comes into play.
Grounded experiences surround us in the mist.
Reality is shady in the darkness.

How can one lose a love that they never possessed?
It carries one mind into a shady future.
It creates a world that exists not.
A mind is trying continually in the darkness.

PARASITES

You are like parasites, eating my brains.
Wormy, wiggly, parasites, nerves of fire.
Parasites breathing and controlling my life.
When you become whole, will you discard me, and I will be no more?

You are like parasites, eating my brains.
Nerves blissful red, crawling more and more.
Sticky parasites are hibernating in every corner of my body.
Popping fire, like rats in the gutter dancing.

You are like parasites, eating my brains.
Like lice itching in my head or mice crawling on my body.
Tapeworms lurch throughout this body.
Maggots' larva, swarming in rotting flesh.

You are like parasites, eating my brains.
As maggots breathe into flies, living on rotten cow head.
There is a constant state of destruction-hatched parasites latched throughout
this body.
Will this mind ever be free?

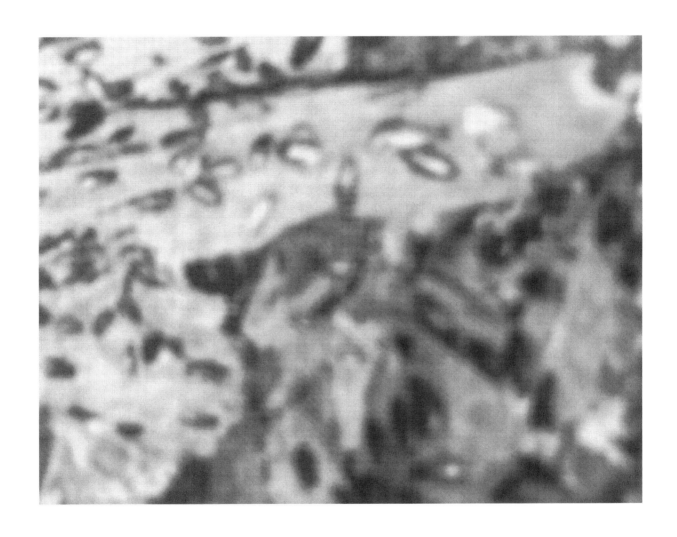

THE PARADOX

The hurt was too deep.
I wanted to kill it.
But, I couldn't without killing the human.
That was the paradox.

The hurt was too deep.
I wanted to kill it.
But I couldn't pay the price to deny self-existence.

The hurt was too deep.
I wanted to kill it.
There was a pill made to escape the depth of this pain.
Maybe, I'm just being vain to think it deserves such credit.

The hurt was too deep.
I wanted to kill it.
But, one day, when I had awakened, my prime lifetime had escaped me.
Because I had buried you, acknowledge you not, perhaps it was my only survival
mode.

HIDDEN INTRUSION

Let me not hide, intrude not.
My thoughts are silent unto me.
Each day I play a role of normality.
I force one foot in front of another.

Let me not hide, intrude not.
I have tried to tame my thoughts into a game of survival.
I have tried not to depart from the lifestyle of my surrounding.
Many days are extraordinary; other days are disturbing.

Let me not hide, intrude not.
There was a hope that the depth of my soul would not show with the road travelers
I met.
I feared the ground would open up and swallow me whole.
My daily journey was not to disappear but to survive.

Let me not hide, intrude not.
Jealous, I stood; happy faces were everywhere.
Chest pains were pressed against me.
Buy me not; I am just trying to survive.

SECRET

Silent agents are hidden deep within a day and night creepers.
What are your hidden agendas?
The silent coffin will call them out, and you will be relieved.
They are the unspeakable ones, the heavy load that floats unrestrained.

Silent agents are hidden deep within a day and night creepers.
I dance in two worlds, living in the present with a loaded past.
Do you?
Tell me your secrets while mine has hung on yonder years.

Silent agents are hidden deep within a day and night creepers.
Will all dare share their secrets?
Secrets holders are windmill twisters.
Twisters are tornados that will destroy all calmness.

Silent agents are hidden deep within a day and night creepers.
Legendary has its own stories and unspoken, hidden secrets.
We dance, and we smile.
Yet, we do not share those deep tree roots.

Silent agents are hidden deep within a day and night creepers.
There are tunnel silent thoughts of what we do not wish to share.
We crawl into our world, not to share what is too painful to bear.
Will the gravesite carve those secrets with our burial?

HAZE

I am in a haze, wholly unable to focus on my clarity.
The dust of smoke surrounds my mind.
With leftover smoke, I cannot move from the past to others.
Your impact has left me with a pearly appearance with others.

I am in a haze, wholly unable to focus on my clarity.
Your relationship left me with a cloudy appearance.
I need to move away from this image, a long-dead relationship.
My mind still hangs on an image that will never be real.

I am in a haze, wholly unable to focus on my clarity.
Morning or night balance you not from my present.
Your puzzle piece has dogmatized me.
Why can't I consciously bury you on a tombstone?

I am in a haze, wholly unable to focus on your clarity.
I am trying to acknowledge the tools to put you at rest.
That is, I must openly deal with my feelings.
To bring you forth, it should not be so painful.

YOUR WAY

It is survival time.
It is about you alone.
Every step, you must breathe life back into yourself.
It would help if you became your universe.

It is survival time.
You must walk the walkway as if you are the only model.
You must please yourself, suspicious or not; it is your survival,
You are in a distrustful state.

It is survival time.
You give little and refuse to take in the gift of another.
Many offer their hearts to you; you take it not.
Knowing one day, you will walk away; you have refused true offered love.

It is survival time.
This atmosphere is too hot; you must create a new one.
Every person must find their road to survive; today, I have chosen mine.
I buried my tracks within the community and left little time for myself.

SMELLING THE GREEN

Decades went by, and I could still smell the green.
It was the day I felt abandoned, a soul torn to pieces.
My new journey did not start with a carousel.
It was a storm left that never seemed to end.

Decades went by, and I could still smell the green.
Left without closure, I bottled it up to face it decades later.
Marry would I, but the dangling past always stood at the door.
Rest me not; the search for a soul went on un-relinquished.

Decades went by, and I could still smell the green.
The gift of home came strong in life.
Many circled me with love and care, but I was their stranger.
I wondered, not that I know; it was a buried coffin in my soul.

Decades went by, and I could still smell the green.
Decades past, faced down, touched me not.
Unsettled thoughts must be arrested.
Green grass must replace the bare empty field.

SECTION IV

CRACKING THE CLOSED CLOSET DOOR

Surviving a lost love meant I had to go into survival mode. Survival mode meant I had to relocate from the West Coast to the East Coast as a VISTA Volunteer, a domestic branch of the Peace Corp. At this time, I had graduated from college and started working towards a graduate degree. My sanity demanded that I move on to maintain my existence. My family was firmly against this move. They had a highly one-sided view of the East Coast, a place infested with rats crawling everywhere. Therefore, none refused to hold their opinion in the rear. I had one supporting auntie, Aunt Everette, who sent me off with her blessings.

I had to relocate because Nathan and Christy had just married. My oldest sister directed their wedding at her church. I wasn't there, of course. I knew his love for Christy was vital because it had survived at least six years. Unfortunately, their marriage lasted only about two years. They had a beautiful girl. This was the same Christy he wrote a poem about and sent to me one month after I had returned to Arkansas from babysitting my first cousin. I had been insane, in short of going to the loony house, thinking a poem was for me when he had someone else's name on it. At the time, I was naïve enough to believe when he explained this name away that he was thinking of me as he wrote the poem.

When I arrived on the East Coast, I was a community organizer stationed in Newark after going through a series of training. I help bring rent control to Newark with other VISTA Volunteers for the first time. Woody was an excellent negotiator.

We, the VISTA Volunteers, walked the steps of the Shudder Home Project, which included twelve levels of floors, with Ellsworth Morgan, our immediate supervisor through VISTA. The elevators were not working most of the time. We worked closely with Helping Hands Welfare Rights Day Care through Janae Day, who was a key figure in assisting Welfare Right Mothers. Every two weeks, the VISTA Volunteers picked up their stipend checks at 33 West Market Street, Old Bethany Baptist Church in Newark, New Jersey, under Rev. James A. Scott. Dr. Scott was closely connected to New York and Washington. He related closely to the VISTA Volunteers. At the time, he was also a Rutgers University professor.

I was too wrapped up with issues in the community to reflect on feeling a sense of self-pity. Being a community organizer kept me constantly busy without the thought of Nathan. I forced my thoughts to go to other issues that demanded immediate action. When that didn't entirely work, I tried to bury the memories of Nathan from my mind by putting them into a grave beyond six feet. I wanted to put those memories into a casket to be buried. I continued to push and push until one day; I realized I must face up to the demon of my past, thereby, the grave memories to be dug up with the loss of my son, Damon.

SECTION IV POEMS

Excavation

My World, My Dream, My Creation

An Eruption

Walls

Loss of Innocence

Mixed Not

Birth Not

What

Trudge

The Postman

Naked Soul

Private Space

Hidden Memories

Procrastination

Wisdom

EXCAVATION

Deep, rooted thoughts, nerves on pin sprouts, you must cry to heal.
Excavation has to come.
Thoughts have simmered into water broil; denied hidden pains must be awakened.
Decades of denial gone must come of age this day.

Deep, rooted thoughts, nerves on pin sprouts, you must cry to heal.
You are out front to hold it together.
The weighted tons are pressing too deep on years gone.
Your outer skin has become stone solid with hidden inner thin paper layers.

Deep, rooted thoughts, nerves on pin sprouts, you must cry to heal.
I don't want to fall, but I am terrified; here me now.
I need to fall, let go and rebuild to heal loads of buried decades.
I hid; I have layered cover sores that have festered over valleys and mountains.

Deep, rooted thoughts, nerves on pin sprouts, you must cry to heal.
How will this day end or the next?
I have survived days gone with brick piles on valley sores.
Will, tomorrow's news read a healing story pushed forward, unlocking the
past?

MY WORLD, MY DREAM,
MY CREATION

My world, my dream, my creation, let it be, let it be.
When reality sets in on you, face it, dismiss it and move on.
Why torment yourself with the elements of life beyond your control?
Life is what it is when it knocks at your door with endless winding roads.

My world, my dream, my creation, let it be, let it be.
Mentally step out and implant a world free from things that tons you down.
It matters only what you see and perceive to control your state of existence.
Let the natural world move on; step off momentarily if you need a break but be
aware.

My world, my dream, my creation, let it be, let it be.
My reality may not be yours, but it is my drumbeat.
It is my chicken coup survival mode.
Give me my crack in the corner, and I will build it to be an open door when the
time comes.

My world, my dream, my creation, let it be, let it be.
There are many drum beaters, but let me be my only wind caller.
The ball of pain will not be in vain because one day, I will pull it together.
The process of cure has begun because the acknowledgment door has been opened.

AN ERUPTION

The hurt couldn't heal because the loss wasn't allowed to occur through
acknowledgment.
Survival was built on falsehood.
The reality was not a part of this functional individual.
Denial was the route of existence.

The hurt couldn't heal because the loss wasn't allowed to occur through
acknowledgment.
Morning and evening were coexistence that carried an element of the past.
A memory that was not allowed to the conscious surface.
When a reckoning day would arrive, the new technique would interplay to push
memory deeper.

The hurt couldn't heal because the loss wasn't allowed to occur through
acknowledgment.
Individual steps would play in my life, but your arm's itch was always hidden in
the event.
High steps would come into my world, and brightness would shine for a few
moments.
How could these moments be so bright and straightforward while the thought of
you would bring me so low?

The hurt couldn't heal because the loss wasn't allowed to occur through
acknowledgment.
You were a love denial syndrome.
A denial syndrome has occupied my life, not allowing me the freedom to live.
Only now, with the recognition of your lost love, I have allowed myself to give
birth to living.

WALLS

I lived and moved on with memories hanging on the walls.
Why did I not learn earlier to put these memories in their place?
Places for future growth, not hind like a runaway slave.
Was it the falsehood of hope that would never come true?

I lived and moved on with memories hanging on the walls.
Yes, I have learned, but it was a great price.
Years of living in the darkness, with hidden conscious thoughts.
Knowing and denying reality is a price paid for not looking in the mirror.

I lived and moved on with memories hanging on the walls.
Where have those memories gone this day?
They have been hidden, locked away.
A door closed so long ago to survive one step at a time.

I lived and moved on with memories hanging on the walls.
Memories unframed clocked closed deep.
A Halloween mask seeking not to be unmasked.
Yet, memories have slowly begun to unmask.

LOSS OF INNOCENCE

Bright sunny clouds have shadows of shades, feeling the loss of a lover so long
ago.
It's the loss of innocence with deep creep memories.
It's the peg on the nerves with pins sticking in the eyes.
Un-controlled mind lost on a merry-go-round.

Bright sunny clouds have shadows of shades, feeling the loss of a lover so long
ago.
There is a desire to control the uncontrollable.
Morning comes with a prescription each day.
Time has strengthened me, but you still run deep.

Bright sunny clouds have shadows of shades, feeling the loss of a lover so long
ago.
I stood on the river edge, watching the tides pound the shore.
What innocent eyes to take in such beauty.
As the surfers ride above the wave, may those innocent eyes never stop glittering.

Bright sunny clouds have shadows of shades, feeling the loss of a lover so long
ago.
Morning has come; it's time for you to leave your box.
Let my mind not wander this day; let it be free for all of me.
It is not you I wish to wander on; I cry for my loss of innocence that came through
you.

MIXED NOT

Had I given myself a mixed message?
It was I who had always craved to be a part of his paved road.
I went with sleepless days and nights that never seemed to end.
His family socked me with his memories that I had already head-packed

Had I given myself a mixed message?
A short moment's release is misread for a lifetime treasure.
Chalk it up; I built a rock out of sand pebbles.
Without an explanation, you disappeared like a magic wand; and I created a sock
of memories that have lingered without your permission.

Had I given myself a mixed message?
With him, it was nothing but a time-release moment.
A moment I carved, stoned, and treasured.
An unknown game played on me over and over again.

Had I given myself a mixed message?
How did I get lost for years in something that never existed?
Lost time, pressure time, a self-created trance, I alone mobilized.
When he was through, he walked and never looked back; I held on.

BIRTH NOT

The beach shores, the movies, or a simple walk in the park never entered our
world.
The birth came forth not.
I know we will never be cemented; I know we will never be cemented as one.
Just as the sunshine lies beneath the icy chills in my body.
Have my memories dissipated themselves?

WHAT

What has come of an old face?
This old face has not changed toward me.
I hear paces of sounds I thought were buried.
Sounds previously echoed have muted to silence.

What has come of an old face?
Words of destruction have come with flush winds.
The guard change has come, pleading for a new me.
Growth is echoing to move forward.

What has come of an old face?
Embarked one has opened up anew.
The news brought openness that dared me not to take it.
That is the new me I have found once buried more profound than a coffin.

What has come of an old face?
A face I cannot dismiss despite my self-destruction.
It is through you that I have opened up about my past.
A new day has truly begun forcing me to deal with past decades.

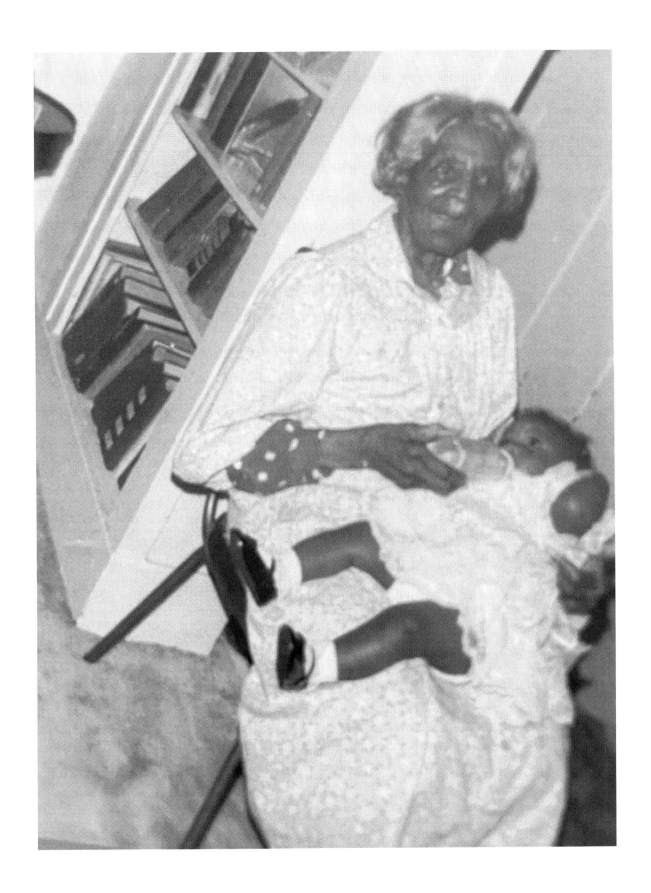

TRUDGE

Family, let the past rest; don't stomp up buried wounds.
Could you have mercy on me?
His name had become malice on your lips.
Please, with a peg in my heart, I beg to let my ears ring free.

Family, let the past rest; don't stomp up buried wounds.
Could you have mercy on me?
I have fought with the pound on my flesh to detangle that summer.
One treasured memory has long sought to be dissipated from the mind.

Family, let the past rest; don't stomp up buried wounds.
Could you have mercy on me?
Desperately, I have repeatedly tried to put those memories to rest.
But at your best, you implanted his name as air fueled from your lungs in my
presence.

Family, let the past rest; don't stomp up buried wounds.
Could you have mercy on me?
Please help me be free from dual complex and painful memories.
Please help me to draw peace and serenity with each step trudging forward.

POSTMAN

The postman came and went.
Wordless, I stood, fighting back an ocean of tears.
The phone rings, and hope rises.
It dwindled as the voice of another was heard.
Fighting back the brisk wind as I walk.
I have desperately tried to rid of old feelings.
They just kept resurfacing.
Had it been puppy love or not?
Maybe it wasn't love.
Maybe it was just an addition to experiencing sex for the first time.

NAKED SOUL

I have loved hard and not so hard.
Were you my first or last?
That is an umbrella fire that holds the heart.
I have loved with great passion, which has ripped my soul naked.

I have loved hard and not so hard.
The nakedness of me has been shown.
I have only once loved unconditionally.
My soul was ripped from my body.

I have loved hard and not so hard.
My eyes have never seen another you.
If you had to replay your role, you would deny me.
You left me with a naked bare soul.

I have loved hard and not so hard.
You gave me love, and I took it graciously.
With and through you, I felt whole as a woman.
Yet, I was not equipped to handle such profound intimacy.

PRIVATE SPACE

There are many emotional levels.
They come with and without tears.
Silence tears, I stand.
The ocean has already overflown.
Silence tears, I stand.
Let me have my private space, with or without tears.

HIDDEN MEMORIES

You were the center of my universe.
What did I do for you to disclaim me?
Picked me apart, little by little, almost destroyed me.
I wondered what I could do to have you again.

You were the center of my universe.
Was I too weak or too strong to leap?
Memories of you had to be suppressed.
Dissipated your memories, my life had to get into control.

You were the center of my universe.
My eyes are open, but they aren't able to see the gift of life.
Eyes are blinded to the beauty of the universe.
There has to be a strength within me to walk that path-way.

You were the center of my universe.
Memories must be buried not to eat me alive.
Your coffin of you has been put in the grave.
That is, the subconscious will take over when you creep to breathe.

PROCRASTINATION

The real world is to separate yesterday's memories.
Memories, I have dragged and swaged into my head for too long.
They were cropped and shopped to fit and mix within my private closet.
It is a full closet, procrastination always standing at the door but cleansing out.

The real world is to separate yesterday's memories.
Memories are bound to one's own-sided views.
Let them not overpower the mind.
Eradicate memories that seek to destroy one's soul.

The real world is to separate yesterday's memories.
Reaping and weeping memories trying to burst out of the closet.
Memories compounded in the head.
Painful memories are trying to elevate themselves.

The real world is to separate yesterday's memories.
Garbage memories need to be cleared.
Buried memories are trying to surface.
The mind is pushing hard to close the closet door.

WISDOM

Wisdom full, I wonder about the experience, the loss of naïve.
How good it felt when innocence walked into me.
It was a lost child in a candy jar.
Brightness, the shining light, carried my feet.

Wisdom full, I wonder about the experience, the loss of naïve.
The innocent time I roamed without a clock.
Separation planted a dominant subconscious in me.
There was no escape; denial played not.

Wisdom full, I wonder about the experience, the loss of naïve.
The innocent replay cannot roll back.
Only mind thoughts can relieve.
Wisdom felt, cry for innocence lost.

Wisdom full, I wonder about the experience, the loss of naïve.
Past innocent joy felt, but the loss was more significant.
You move; you carry on. That's life.
The Past is rooted with strands, but you must last and walk another day.

SECTION V

MOVES TO EXECRATE SELF

Yet, reality kept coming back, memories, and memories. To move on, I had to deal with losing my innocence beyond trying to bury it.

I moved on with two brief marriages. Each one was a marriage for a lifetime in my mind initially. Willie was a wonderful person, yet he had a significant challenge. He was tied to his family, as was I, but he had additional problems. He was a weekend alcoholic. I left within two years; he filed for divorce three years later. My second marriage lasted less than one year in 1985. I sought a divorce from Emmanuel. I can only say that the condition of my mind played a significant role in those two marriages. My mind had begun to develop into a state of stability. I began to search the inner me accepting what would remain within my heart but moving forward with my inner spirit. The second marriage should have never taken place. He had one purpose in mind, his citizenship, and I had a lifetime marriage. I became aware of this, ended our marriage immediately, and moved on. My first step was to seek out Nathan to face him one-on-one. During so, I knew that Nathan's wedding had ended two years after he had married Christy. Nathan and his former wife had had a beautiful baby girl.

I flew to California, spent one night with Nathan, took him out to breakfast the next morning, and flew back to the East Coast the same day. I called Nathan two days later and asked him what he was doing for the evening. He said, "I don't know what you are doing, but I am, going to San Francisco to hang out for the evening," I said, "Okay, bye." And he said, "Bye." I can say genuinely that I closed the door on a casket that day. Although Nathan had closed the door on me the summer, I returned home to Arkansas to finish high school. Perhaps, Nathan never had me in his doorway. I probably was one within the treasure box that he masturbated with when his needs arrived. I have never spoken to Nathan since that day. When we finally crossed paths again, one of his brothers, a retired judge, said to me, "Let me marry you and Nathan; just say yes." I looked at his brother and spoke not a word. First, I was there with my present husband, which was disrespectful.

I have come into my being, my whole being, as a human being. This is me, who has faced my great demon, Nathan, because I have allowed it to be. Yet, I should be thankful in a way.

Because of Nathan, I relocated to the East Coast and later adopted two sons. One who is recently deceased, whose death I have yet not entirely accepted. Yet, his strength assisted me in putting my collective thoughts in order of my mast. Each time Nathan had risen into my mind, I had set my pen to work; it had been my survival mode.

My sanity has been my pen. Without it, I may have become a homeless person on the street. Therefore, we always acknowledge an actual homeless person because one never knows the treasure of a lifestyle based on life events. Perhaps, I would have fallen into the latter category. I can credit my fat, who had instilled within me to find modes of self-survival when your life holds onto a thread hanging off a cliff. Everyone has ways of self-survival; there is not one particular tool that will work for everyone. Each person must find their survival tool. The pen has been mine. It has allowed me to pour out the depth of my deepest subconscious thoughts about Nathan; it has been my actual counselor. Damon, my son, your wounds are too open for a band aide.

One day, I hope to begin that long walk down the corridor, healing and losing your presence here on earth. Although you are gone, you and one encouraging remark made by Henrietta have played a significant role in collecting my decades of work on Nathan to share my healing. God has angels to show up when you need one.

SECTION V
POEMS

The Ceiling

Empty Closet

Buried

Toxic

Released

The Great Smile

Fantasy

Cats Love

Beyond Teased

New Light

Dormant

Wisdom Age

Depleted Hope Check

The Pen

THE CEILING

The tools are hidden.
They are bound in me.
Why can't I climb that ladder?
Yet, I'm here wallowing on the floor.

The tools are hidden.
Could it be me structured out of my lane?
Have I not wallowed in self-pity too long?
Is this not a body that has been isolated into a skeleton?

The tools are hidden.
Do I inch to the ladder and climb?
Or do I continue to dig a hole and cry with memories?
What do I choose?

The tools are hidden.
When you inch not, your emotions stay fresh.
You may not get the ceiling, but you can reach a beach.
Let it not be five decades later.

EMPTY CLOSET

Emotions must be shared openly, not buried.
If not, a stagnated mind grows not.
As a full closet empty of clothes to wear.
Let them not be roaming eyes to see a full moon with the sky covered with
clouds.

BURIED

A buried coffin within me waited to be excavated to life.
When you left without an explanation, it was beyond my psycho level.
I felt dirty, unclean, unwanted, and without life; you were the first to explore the innocent pure.
A cannon built to fire was now ice cold.

A buried coffin within me waited to be excavated to life.
You were always the overcast in a life that never was or would be.
When your surface had risen, the slug hammer became my survival tool; I routed you deeper.
When you yoked your mate, the other side of the world became my home.

A buried coffin within me waited to be excavated to life.
Years later, I sought you out; you received me again for a night of pleasure and release.
A reckon time had to come upon me, this I knew.
Like a snail, I returned to my shell, a life I knew would go on forever without you.

A buried coffin within me waited to be excavated to life.
Life is what it is, and we must all learn to live with the reality of it.
I have learned the excavation step.
A buried coffin within me waits no more; this is me, an opened book.

TOXIC

Were you toxic to my life?
Perhaps that's not the question to ask.
Did I have the experience to embark upon such a relationship?
Perhaps that is the question.

Were you toxic to my life?
Through you, my eyes were opened to feel the depth of love.
So how can I feel those moments when I am sane?
Although the pain of losing you became a legacy within my life.

Were you toxic to my life?
The new relationship was sought through your experiences.
Did they not have a chance to place a footprint in the sand with me?
Perhaps Judgement Day had come before even a new hello.

Were you toxic to my life?
Perhaps I placed myself in toxicity.
A city of ruins, eyelid garbage diced with drugs and alcohol.
How can that be with a cleansed body?

Were you toxic to my life?
The body dances with the mental state of mind.
How did so many years escape with you sitting at my head table?
My head table always had your arms resting, and I was not even a ghost in your
memory.

RELEASED

I often think of you, knowing I mattered not even as an ant within your world.
Why is this possible?
Knowing the lack of our original separation, the thought of you should be a distant
world apart of mine.
I have just allowed you to run loose wild in my mind at times.

I often think of you, knowing I mattered not even as an ant within your world.
Perhaps it is the lack of freedom I have over my mind.
Your world is a distance apart from me.
I must release you; the willingness has to come.

I often think of you, knowing I mattered not even as an ant within your world.
The ability to love another or fantasize came through you.
It is a perfect utopic place that I created.
A fantasy, be it true or not.

I often think of you, knowing I mattered not even as an ant within your world.
How has this day come for me to release you?
The legacy of you has come knowing you have impacted my life.
It is time to be free and see the real sunny flowers of others.

THE GREAT SMILE

Your smile has left pure thoughts of you with me.
I wish I could say I'm over you, but your smile will always remain implanted in
my mind.
Many decades have come and gone with dissipated relationship thinking and
wanting you.
Could it be that you left me without a word or closer, or you never entered my
world?

Your smile has left pure thoughts of you with me.
I knew it was my fantasy of having you that I own, with your lasting implanted
smile on me.
Only now can I release myself from the prison of wanting you.
It was that day I had begun sharing you openly with me.

Your smile has left pure thoughts of you with me.
Finally, am I over you?
When I close my eyes, I see me, not you, my new fantasy.
The sun filled with the faces of others.

Your smile has left pure thoughts of you with me.
Your smile has left pure thoughts of you with me.
I can acknowledge you and my fantasy of you without shame.
I have learned to accept life and move forward without your thoughts controlling
me.

FANTASY

A fantastic fantasy, and you are absent.
A family with all the trimming moves gloriously happily.
How can that be?
Without you, it is an unbelievable reality.

A fantastic fantasy, and you are absent.
A family that is full of children with all their needs being met.
I never brought one forth but claimed two, non-womb pop.
Can a fantasy of six fix what I do not have in my ring?

A fantastic fantasy, and you are absent.
The fantasy brings me into a perfect arena without a thought of you.
How time can change with decades on my shoulders.
Youth imagination, this day, could have never brought my mind here.

A fantastic fantasy, and you are absent.
Please do not knock on my institutional door because I am fully aware of my
fantasy.
Let me have my fantasy of living within a perfect circle.
Perfect moment, isolated moment, free of all, utopic it was, let it not be gone.

CATS' LOVE

Oliver, it was called, or was it, princess?
Cats are just names to me; she wanted me to caress them like a lost love.
Hugs and kisses, she embraced them both like none other.
They danced, ran, and played with balls in those narrow halls.

Oliver, it was called, or was it, princess?
Fantasy love stokes never prove to be a reality.
The eyes brought back sought love that never entered pure reality.
She pressed and caressed their fury body gently against her soft skin.

Oliver, it was called, or was it, princess?
She embraced their fuzzy, hairy fur as I had wished to capture a lost lover.
Each stroke was effectively placed on their early soft fur.
A distance sought love encountered that mindless stroke.

Oliver, it was called, or was it, princess?
Pure, innocent love displayed. With care, they were surrounded by such envy.
This world should not bear; allow me to function free this day.
This pure bountiful cat's love, jealous I should encounter not.

BEYOND TEASED

They teased and mocked me after years gone, so many years stolen.
What pleasure did they receive from such demise?
Were their worlds limited that they had to seek to destroy?
Has my humanity not honored them on a level gone?

They teased and mocked me after years gone, so many years stolen.
Old with wrinkles stand this day.
Youth has tickled me for years.
My heart with virginity has been stolen, but wise, I stand this day.

They teased and mocked me after years gone, so many years stolen.
Through them, I have awakened on lost years.
That, it was not meant to be!
My demise agony was their content.

They teased and mocked me after years gone, so many years stolen.
The growth I stand this day, beyond the torment you sought.
Have five lost decades gone not enough?
Age has not kindled your spirit.

They teased and mocked me after years gone, so many years stolen
Have you not pitied that pained heart that has pounded in vain?
Separated distance from others sought a cure.
Your memories work not from this day forward; buried pains are opened for a
cure.

THE LIGHT

Is it true that a thin line lies between love and hate?
That, I cannot tell.
Love never died for you, even in your absence.
I was missing you endlessly with a buried denial that I had stone solid caged.

Is it true that a thin line lies between love and hate?
That, I cannot tell.
The raft of your deeds never took the thought of you away.
You have ridden amid others I could not control or patrol you away.

Is it true that a thin line lies between love and hate?
That, I cannot tell.
My pain is not your pain, and I am sure you do not wish it upon me.
The gift of growth is having the maturity of forgiveness.

Is it true that a thin line lies between love and hate?
That, I cannot tell.
This awareness is much too late, but it has come.
New life, new birth has opened a force of a bright light unto me.

DORMANT

All fresh, old, whole, and new have come out in the birth of openness.
Buried thoughts are no more, I feel fresh, but the stain still has it tame.
You have impacted thoughts.
Pure and anxious wounds have flushed pounds.

All fresh, old, whole, and new have come out in the birth of openness.
When will it all emerge into one and be no more?
Bits and pieces have picked me apart.
I want to be whole in me.

All fresh, old, whole, and new have come out in the birth of openness.
The drummer and the beater took an old tune to create a new beat to meet one's needs.
It is an old beat, but it had a flare that set a fire and couldn't be distinguished.
It is an open pit with splinters kindling the fire not.

All fresh, old, whole, and new have come out in the birth of openness.
A new life has moved forward with the discovery of uncovered stone.
Uncovered stones have lain dormant for years.
Stones glassed into pebbles, searching and ready to become whole in oneself.

WISDOM AGE

Don't look at me strangely; I know it should not be decades.
With a gouging open vein, I'm just trying to recover.
I've been through hurt and pain.
Young eyes, honor the pain, and move on; let age be not your wisdom.

Don't look at me strangely; I know it should not be decades.
It creates a brief moment of pleasure by running, not acknowledging it.
I am getting a moment high, like playing the casino, losing by the millions.
The hoarder, shopping to save when modern, has become an outdated junk mess.

Don't look at me strangely; I know it should not be decades.
What you see, let it be a lesson learned not to duplicate.
In life, we all have a place in the puzzle; unless you are an exceptional human
being, perhaps you are.
To have truly loved and lost is a lesson for a lifetime; recognize it, accept it and
deal with it to move on.

Don't look at me strangely; I know it should not be decades.
This is my comment of reflection; let it be not yours.
: et my few strands of thread be your guide to complete a garment.
Cement yourself in the present, live not in the past and use it as a guide to creating
anew.

DEPLETED HOPE CHEST

Perhaps I needed to lose to have eyes to see.
Yet, the loss of you has made me a writer.
Stills the void feels more profound than a bombing gushing a hold in the earth.
My eyes have seen the redness of the sea.

Perhaps I needed to lose to have eyes to see.
My eyes have cried, wanting to want of you.
I was in your world that I could see.
The faucet continued to drip, drip, endlessly.

Perhaps I needed to lose to have eyes to see.
My blindness carried me into a senseless nothing.
Although, to this day, I stand marvelously well.
Firmly, I stand.

Perhaps I needed to lose to have eyes to see.
My world has never stopped.
You just stopped loving me and moved on.
Yet, you stayed in my hope chest until it depleted itself.

THE PEN

I write for survival and life.
It takes me where my pen must save me.
The pen occupies the space where there is not a here or there.
It comes along to take me out of orbit.

I write for survival and life.
It demands me to cope.
It has its space; not to lose me, I must acknowledge a sense of its control in me.
I can't lose it; if it goes, perhaps my thoughts would mingle and jingle into orbit.

I write for survival and life.
It has space, not constant free, with a deep corner connected with me.
Jump, run, always in my head, open dancing alone.
Dancing along, embraced by none, not even me, until my pen takes ownership.

I write for survival and life.
I write to escape, cope, coping with braises in my brains.
Sometimes it disappears, returns to me, and wants my last breath.
I pen it away until hibernation time is up and the closed closet door opens again.

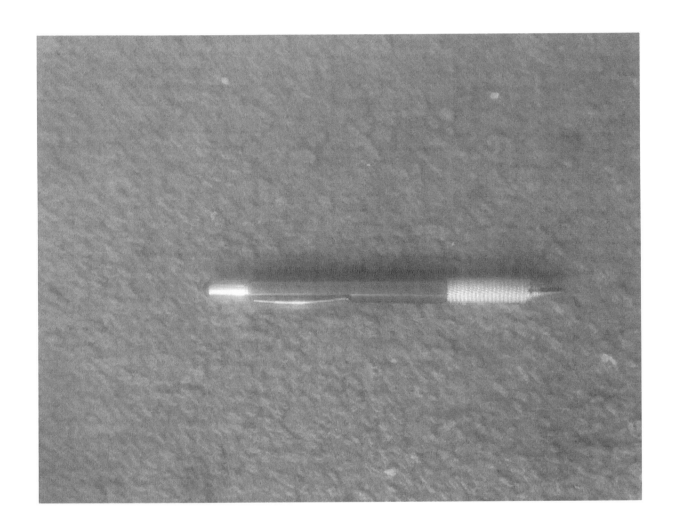

SECTION VI

THE SUN IS JUST BENEATH THE CLOUD

One should never forget to view and control the destiny that lies in front of their feet. There is a brighter light for each individual that may temporarily stand within the dimness of darkness. There will always be a rainbow of colors waiting to be received.

SECTION VI
POEMS

Love Image

Who Was I

Entitlement

Honoring Pain

Recognition

LOVE IMAGE

Beauty is just a time element that will one day disappear as we see it.
We look at one's face, shape, hair, or smile, which we see to take upon our love.
We fantasize about one shape, whether small or large; it is what we desire at the time.
Do we ever look beyond the shape that pulls us toward another?

Beauty is just a time element that will one day disappear as we see it.
We define one as tall and handsome with a striking pose.
A lover once said, "It was her knotted cropped knitted closely to her head that magnetized me."
Society has conditioned us to view live images rather than beauty.

Beauty is just a time element that will one day disappear as we see it.
How does one cope when love is just an image of society?
Society will determine your mate if you focus only on what has been the image cultivated in your mind.
Let society not control your mate through images.

Beauty is just a time element that will one day disappear as we see it.
Look beyond images to ask how and why I fell in love.
Let it not be the twinkle in one's eye.
Walk and embrace the commonality of each one's thoughts.

WHO WAS I?

I did not disappear through the sour of another.
One day I went walking and saw myself.
I Once was a zombie.
I mumbled and fumbled among the streets.

I did not disappear through the sour of another.
My mind appeared to be gone with the absence of you.
I pinched the air to find a human touch but found the bareness of me.
The stain of the pain found a way out.

I did not disappear through the sour of another.
I had chosen not the un-bind road.
The goodness of man saw a bright star in me.
My steps were taken from homeless streets.

I did not disappear through the sour of another.
Although my shoulders were stressed and pressed at times, I moved on.
There was a stride out in my walk that gave me hope.
Yes, I did not disappear through the sour of another.

SECTION VI

ENTITLEMENT

You are entitled to fall in and out of love.
But be gentle with the breakup when you have been the first.
You can be firm with an appreciation of the experience.
Was that too much to ask of you?

You are entitled to fall in and out of love.
You get a pass for the freedom to love with your conscious.
Yet, you don't get a pass for disregarding another's feelings.
I shared your intimacy, which deserves a respectful department unless you are less than.

You are entitled to fall in and out of love.
Nothing is more significant than sharing the intimacy of another, combined as one.
With you, I felt the epitome of love, two as one, but it was not to last.
You were not connected in that same arena as I.

You are entitled to fall in and out of love.
After you, I always was on guard not to mislead another.
I became too continuous to clarify my future relationship.
You were my greatest love and my most significant handicap to love another.

HONORING PAINS

At times the element of being whole is so painful.
It is the process of opening up oneself raw.
It is the ability to honor one past with all its issues.
The dark vomit issues of one's life come out.

At times the element of being whole is so painful.
You begin opening the casket that has been lain buried for years gone.
The door that was forced shut you have opened.
Deadbolt steel locks are difficult to open.

At times the element of being whole is so painful.
One's past wrongs come to light.
The fragility and weakness of one are undertaken.
To have moved forward to the light has gone raw into my soul.

At times the element of being whole is so painful.
Pent-up nerves must itch out for the freedom to live whole.
'The mind must dance to unlock that door.
Honoring the pain is to release it.

RECOGNITION

It was moving, holding on to the old and the new.
It's a new me.
Loving and hurting, uncluttering doors, it's me.
Crawling, making inches into steps, I'm reaching for the mountain.
It's me, just trying to be whole.

OUR WEDDING CEREMONY

**THE MARRIAGE SERVICE
OF
OLLIE MARSHALL
AND
LUIS ALONSO TREJO RICO
SATURDAY, MARCH 8, 2003
11:00 A.M.**

PRELUDE

LIGHTING OF THE CANDLES

SOLO—YOU LIGHT UP MY LIFE
JUNE LOCKETT

PROCESSIONAL

AIR ON A STRING
T. S. BACH

BRIDAL MARCH
RICHARD WAGNER

PRESENTATION OF THE BRIDE

SCRIPTURE
1 CORINTHIANS 13
SLYVESTER LUCAS

EXCHANGE OF VOWS

EXCHANGE OF RINGS

LIGHTING THE UNITY CANDLE

PRAYER

SOLO——THE LORD'S PRAYER
JUNE LOCKETT

PRONOUNCEMENT

PRESENTATION—MR. & MRS. LUIS RICO

RECESSIONAL

THE WEDDING PARTY

ORGANISTS

REV FRANK WALTERS

LYDIA MATHIS

MAID OF HONOR

BEATRICE MARSHALL

BEST MAN

RAMOR TREJO

USHERS

MALCOLM HAYMAN
KATIE ROBINSON
NADINE SKIPWITH
AMELIA WELCH
PRESTLY WOOD

CANDLE LIGHTERS

EVERETTE PIERSON
ANGELIA RICO

DIRECTRESS

CORINE LUCAS

GUEST BOOK

KATIE WALDROP

GIFT TABLE

VICTORIA BRITT

HOST/HOSTESS

TIMMESHA BROWN
VALISHA MARSHALL
BERRY MARSHALL

SPECIAL THANKS TO SAMUEL,
SIRRINA, SABRINA WALDROP AND
CALVIN MARSHALL

RECEPTION IMMEDIATELY FOLLOWIING
CEREMONY

BETHANY BAPTIST CHURCH
275 WEST MARKET STREET
NEWARK, NEW JERSEY 07103

Book Cover

Ollie takes us on a personal journey within the book "Surviving the Stain of Losing My First Love." She leaves nothing unanswered in sharing the naked truth of her loss. She subconsciously realized she was one of many in a treasure box to whom she released her virginity. Still, unfortunately, she buries that truth with her inability to cope. She relocated to the opposite of the world when he married, knowing escape was only her survival mode.

Decades later, she is forced to come to grips with the perception of love that she experienced at eighteen when she lost her virginity. She knows everyone is responsible for following their hearts wherever it takes them. Her only pounding thoughts are, why didn't he take a better road in dealing with her feelings? She saw the sun through his eyes; his stars were her moving glory. The truth and the lack of facts were all the same when it came from his mouth that he knew. Perhaps she knew the difference too when they had sprung from his lips, but the trail of her effective for him would only move as he dictated.

It was five decades since she was pounded with his loss until the death of her oldest son. She had to dig up the grave of her first loss to survive her son's loss. As painful as it was, this journey had to be taken without a choice.

If there is a lesson from Ollie's story, everyone has a right to follow their own heart but travel softly with those you meet on the way, especially if you are the first to steal their virginity. The question still pounds within her heart how can one genuinely fall in love if they are constantly evaluating on the edge of being cautious? Because there is an element of a man whose needs are based upon selflessness. We each seek the perfect mate, but in reality, is there one? Let the stone speak.

Stone
A stone knocked on my door yesterday.
I let it in because I thought it was cotton.
It meshed me into pieces; perhaps it did not even know.
It became the last as well as the first.
Innocent eyes were hopeless, casket closed.
The stone left a life's tone with its own set of memories.

The Bed

…
There were days the bed became my savior.
Reality came, and I proceeded with life.
Each step became a journey.
Tasks of survival moved on with mandatory chores.
…

Yes, it was hard holding on day by day. I had pride within myself but couldn't turn Nathan's thoughts away. A time that laid buried until this day…this is my naked rawness.

Made in the USA
Middletown, DE
05 March 2023

26166002R00082